WORLD SOCCER SKILL

by Dave Spurdens

STUDIO PUBLICATIONS
IPSWICH, ENGLAND

First published in 1979
This edition published 1987 by
Studio Publications (Ipswich) Ltd,
The Drift, Nacton Road, Ipswich, England

CONTENTS

INTRODUCTION

by Dave Spurdens

The pace of life, the materialist society, mass production, they have it seems, touched all aspects of the world we live in. Football, no less than other facets, has fallen prey to these menaces. Managers and coaches at professional level would all like a greater freedom of expression but they are forced to bow to the greater gods of our existence . . . the balance sheet, the trophy cupboard, the satisfied and largely parochial public.

We cannot argue that this is a global trend, it is not. Some of the most exciting creative soccer ever seen has been played over the last fifteen years by South American and Continental teams.

It is hoped this book will stimulate a reawakening of our love of individuality.

The Continentals have, I feel, not been fully converted to the sophistication of modern coaching development, and have stayed closer to the natural explorative learning situation which goes with a back alley and a tennis ball. This has passed from our game and, in copying the overall patterns of our league teams, young players in England have emerged with a limited range of things they can do with a ball in any given situation. To fill this void, as well as to positively develop an exciting new attitude towards ball mastery, is the province of this book. I would not pretend that all these skills would become a predominant feature of any player's repertoire, though to a great extent it will depend on the level of expertise achieved. But the magic moments, the flashes of individuality, are the memorable crumbs in a very staple diet, and without them the ethos of the game becomes tarnished to the point of ordinariness.

A principle of educational thinking over the last century has been the belief that to develop the man in a comprehensive sense, exposing him to all facets of knowledge, will equip him more fully for the choice and decisions which lay before him. I have adhered to my own firm belief — that this is the only viable principle on which an open minded, receptive society can be built — in presenting this book in relation to the more precise aspirations of this particular sport. The more comprehensive our range of skills, the more conversant we are with our capacity to respond to given situations in a variety of ways, then the more likely we are to raise the standard of our game to a sublime level, while the opposite is true if we hold back from this fertile area of exploration and experimentation.

Over the years I have realised there is a gulf of interpretation between what a player *thinks* makes up the mechanics of a skill and what actually takes place. One particular skill in this, The Keegan, was the subject of an experiment I conducted with three separate groups of boys. The groups were in three age ranges, 10—12, 12—14 and 14—17 years. I demonstrated the skill and asked them in turn to reproduce what I had just done. Nobody managed to reproduce the skill. With each round of failure I demonstrated the skill again at a realistic speed. It was after six demonstrations that I broke the skill down into parts and subsequently everybody in the group began to reproduce the skill at a reasonable level. This, I believe, demonstrates the need for a specific skill suggestion programme which separates the various mechanical stages of a skill.

Coaches, managers and teachers, may like to conduct their own experiments but I have found that the response made by young players to negotiating skill problems is invariably an orthodox one. Put out a row of skittles with two-metre gaps and the player will weave through them using the inside of both feet. It has to be suggested to him that there are numerous combinations of surfaces and techniques which he could use, e.g., outside and inside of one foot, outsides of both feet, sole roll and outside of one foot, sole roll and outside of both feet, sole roll, toe roll, mobile juggle permutating the surfaces, backwards toe pull, and so on.

The same applies to other skill problems; throw a high ball and it is invariably trapped using the inside instep surface or by bringing the sole down on top of the ball. Hit a ball along the ground and predictably it will be the inside instep with which it will be controlled, whereas the responses that could have been made are numerous.

There is another reason for compiling a book of this kind which has nothing to do with reality, utility or productivity. That reason is enjoyment. The pure, uninhibited, unashamed enjoyment of playing with a ball and gradually asserting ones influence over the wayward idiosyncrasies of that troublesome sphere, about which we all get so excited.

1. DRIBBLING SKILLS

1 THE KEEGAN
STEP-OVER

This skill can be executed standing still or on the run. The leading foot is brought explosively over the ball passing from outside to inside giving the impression that a diagonal shot is being attempted. Having touched down just inside the ball, the outside of the foot sweeps the ball to the outside of the player, ready for a shot, a pass or to continue the run. An ideal skill for clearing an opening for a shot.

1 The player must be chest on to the ball with the ball in front of the controlling foot.

2 The controlling foot is moved swiftly over the ball from outside to inside. The whole body must intimate that a shot or pass is about to be made.

3 The controlling foot must touch the ground beyond the ball and to the inside of it.

4 Using the outside of the foot, the ball is swept outside of the normal line of the controlling leg.

5 Done properly the way should now be clear for advancement.

2 THE KEEGAN
OUTSIDE FOOT FLICK

The Keegan dummy is described in the previous skill. In this skill when the foot has passed over the ball and landed to the inside of it the player swivels explosively on the heel flicking the ball with the outside of the foot to a point diagonally or immediately behind him.

1 The foot is passed explosively over the top of the ball from outside to inside.

2 The foot which is now on the ground is swivelled outwards and backwards on the heel with the outside area of the foot making contact with the ball.

3 As the foot swivels on the heel so the body pivots round to the direction of the pass.

4 This skill is most useful when a player is being driven away from his objective, as a means of turning to beat a player or setting up a wall pass situation.

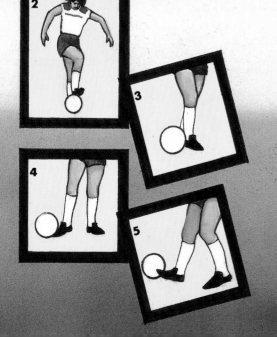

3 THE ROSSI
BACK FOOT DRAG

Often when faced with an agile and alert opponent our dummies and feints do not work and we find him still in the same position as he was before the dummy. This skill is particularly useful as a compensatory manoeuvre for this eventuality.

The dummy is executed as in The Keegan Skill. After the dummying foot has passed over the ball the back foot drags through with the outside instep making contact with the ball and knocking it on in front of the original dummying foot. As was stated earlier, if an opponent has remained unmoved by a deception this follow-up ploy may well leave him standing.

1 The player must be chest-on to the ball with the ball in front of the controlling foot.

2 The controlling foot is propelled swiftly over the ball from outside to inside. The whole body must intimate that a shot or pass is about to be made.

3 The controlling foot must touch the ground beyond the ball and to the inside of it.

4 At this point with the dummying foot beyond and inside the ball the back foot is dragged through to the ball playing it with the outside and upper surface and pushing it forward.

5 Acceleration is important now and a good running pattern must be established quickly.

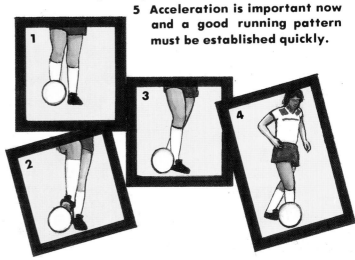

4 THE ROSSI
REVERSE STEP-OVER

In this skill the leading foot is brought explosively across the top of the ball from inside to outside and the ball swept inside using the instep.

1 The player must be chest on to the ball with the ball in front of the controlling foot.

2 The controlling foot is pushed quickly over the ball from inside to outside the ball. The whole body must intimate that an outside of the foot pass is about to be made.

3 The controlling foot must touch down beyond the ball and to the outside of it.

4 Using the inside of the dummying foot the ball is swept inwards in the direction of the standing foot.

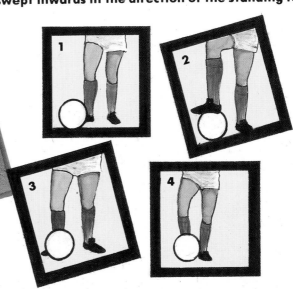

5 THE CRUYFF

This skill differs from the previous skill in that the dummy is not explosive because we do not want it to be 'bought'. After the foot has passed over the ball from inside to outside the player continues in the same direction as the dummy, taking the ball with him, using the inside surface of the other foot.

1. **Execute the Rossi Reverse Step-over as described but do not make the dummy an explosive one.**

2. **Body weight will have been transferred to the dummying foot and this momentum should be continued.**

3. **The ball should now be pushed across the dummying foot with the other foot using the inside surface of the instep.**

4. **Acceleration is now the key factor, having wrong footed your opponent in this way.**

6 THE SOCRATES

The Rossi dummy described previously is the first part of this skill. The sole pull is added to the dummy after the foot has passed over the ball from the inside to the outside. The sole of the dummying foot pulls the ball back inside, across the standing foot.

1. **Dummy to push the ball with the outside of the foot but pass the foot over the top of the ball. The foot should touch down just to the outside of the ball.**

2. **The trunk should be moved to suggest that the player intends to take the ball to his outside.**

3. **The sole of the dummying foot is now placed on top of the ball and rolled across the top dragging the ball inside and across the standing foot.**

VARIATION

Where an opponent has not been fooled by the ploy, the ball can be switched back across the original playing foot with the instep of the original standing foot.

THE KEEGAN ROSSI
COMBINATION

This is a compound skill where the two previously described ploys, numbers 1 and 4, are put together to form a dribbling movement. They can be linked together in either sequence. Where the Keegan is used first the sequence is foot over ball from outside to inside moving the ball to a position outside the player, the same foot then passes over the ball from inside to outside before sweeping the ball inwards, towards or past the standing foot.

1 **The components are a combination of Skill numbers 1 to 4 put together in whichever order is appropriate.**

THE CONTI

This skill can be used to attack the opponents goal after being forced in the opposite direction by a close marking defender. The player, moving in one direction will feign to make a diagonal run in the opposite direction to which he intends to go; turns the ball back inside his standing foot turning in the opposite direction to collect the ball and make for goal.

1 **The player has his back to the target and is moving away from it.**

2 **He pivots on the standing foot at the same time as playing the ball with the inside toe area of the controlling foot.**

3 **The ball is played inside the standing foot and in the opposite direction to the dummy made earlier.**

4 **The player then turns; e.g., if the ball is turned with the left foot then the player will turn to the right.**

5 **At the time of turning the ball and himself the player is balanced on the ball of the standing foot.**

9 THE CONTI
PASS RECEIVED AND TURN

The player receives the pass with his back facing the target he hopes to realise. The pass is collected by the receiving foot and turned inside the standing foot. Swivel takes place on the standing foot preceding the poing of contact; after the ball has been turned inside the standing foot the swivel continues so that the player is facing in the opposite direction, where he collects the ball.

1 The player faces the incoming pass which needs to be on the ground before the skill can be considered.

2 On receiving the ball within range of the playing foot the player swivels on the standing foot making contact with the outside of the ball with the inside of the playing foot.

3 The ball is redirected inside the standing foot.

4 The player continues to swivel on the standing foot complete a half, or slightly more than a half turn.

5 He then collects the ball with the same foot as used originally to receive the ball at the outset.

10 THE CONTI
BALL THROUGH LEGS AND TURN

In the Conti dribble the player has possession of the ball before performing the skill. In this skill the ball is passed to him and gives the impression of having passed between his legs before turning it back inside his standing leg.

1 The player receives the pass and turns his back to the passer at the last minute. He must watch the ball throughout.

2 The player allows the ball to pass between his legs but no further than the playing foot.

3 At this point the ball is turned back inside the standing foot in the direction from which it came.

4 At the same time as (3) is performed the player swivels on the standing foot, e.g., if the right foot is used to play the ball the left foot swivels, with the heel moving inwards.

THE FALCAO
STEP-OVER AND RIDE

This skill is a combination of a dummy and a pace absorber. The player approaches the oncoming ball sideways on; the leading leg is extended over the ball explosively to feign an outside of the foot pass; the ball is allowed to run to the inside of the back foot which gives with the pace, riding round with the ball as the player pivots on the front foot.

1. **The player approaches the ball sideways on.**

2. **The foot nearest the ball dummies to kick with the outside of the foot, but passes over the top of the ball.**

3. **The ball follows through to the inside foot surface of the back foot.**

4. **The pivot on the front foot begins at the moment of contact between the back foot and the ball causing the back foot to guide the ball round in a U shape.**

THE SOUNESS

This skill is used when a player is being 'closed down' by his opponent. The players legs are apart with the ball in a central position. The player rocks from one foot to the other. The last foot touches down close to the ball. Several changes of direction may have to be made before an opponent makes his move. The ball is played to take advantage of an opponents momentary shift.

1. **The ball is on the ground. The players feet are apart with the ball between them.**

2. **The player rocks from side to side shifting off one foot and moving it away from the ball, moving the inside of the other foot to the side of the ball.**

3. **The trunk and head make a pronounced feint as though the ball is to be played across the standing foot.**

4. **If the opponent moves to cover the feint then it is the inside of the standing foot which comes across and plays the ball in the opposite direction.**

5. **Several movements from side to side may have to be made before an opponent commits himself.**

13 THE VAN der ELST

This skill has all round movement opportunities and allows change of control to take place very quickly. The ball is pulled in different directions using the sole of the foot. The player must synchronize body movement with the movement of the ball otherwise loss of balance occurs.

1 The movement is best started with the ball at extended leg distance from the player.

2 The player pulls the ball towards him and moves to the side of the ball keeping the same distance between himself and the ball so as to be able to pull the ball into himself again.

3 This routine continues with the player pulling the ball through to himself at a variety of angles.

4 The pulling movements can be continuous or the ball can be stopped with the inside or outside of the foot.

5
The pull does not have to be straight back towards the player, it can be pulled sideways, stroking the foot across the top of the ball from outside to inside.

3 Push the ball forward and outside the second playing foot.

4 Take the body across to the position it occupied in (1) and repeat this zig-zag movement until the pattern is established.

14 *BOTH OUTSIDE FOOT SURFACES*

An important feature of dribbling skills is rhythm. Good rhythm needs good balance and the poise to change direction swiftly and quickly. In this skill the outside surface of both feet is alternated to provide the forward momentum necessary for a positive dribble.

If, for example, the dribble is started with the right foot the ball is pushed to the front and outside of the player using the outside surface. The body is then brought across the ball so that it is to the outside of the left foot, the ball is then pushed to the front and outside by the left foot.

1 Push the ball, using the outside foot surface to the front of and outside the playing foot.

2 Bring the body across the ball so that the other foot has the ball to its outside.

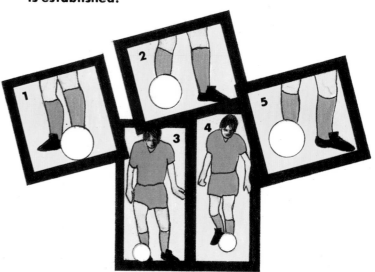

THE PLATINI

BACKWARD TOE ROLL

Often we are forced by opponents to go backwards while in possession. Usually we try to do this by keeping our body between the ball and the opponent. There are occasions, however, when we want to tempt opponents to 'bite' at the ball to create the space and opportunity to get beyond him. In this skill the ball is dragged backwards using the toe area of the sole.

1 **Place the toe area of the sole on the uppermost point of the ball.**

2 **Pulling the foot backwards towards oneself we place the playing foot back on the ground after each movement.**

3 **Because so much of this activity is on one foot the arms play an important role in stabilising the body.**

VARIATION
After pulling the ball backwards several times it is advisable to link this to a forward movement so that a pattern of reverse action can be established.

THE ARDILES

This skill is used a lot for pulling the ball wide of a player coming in to tackle from the front. The player running with the ball leans his body to one side away from the playing foot. Just before an attack he pulls the ball wide towards the standing foot or beyond it with the sole of his foot rolling sideways across the top of the ball.

1 **Take the ball forward to an opponent preferably using the outside of the foot.**

2 **Dummy to go even further to the outside just before reaching the opponent.**

3 **With the player off balance pull the ball inside towards the standing foot using the sole.**

4 **By dragging the sole across the top of the ball and slightly down its outside surface the ball will roll across the playing foot and beyond the standing foot.**

17 THE DALGLISH

This particular trick can be used as a means of thwarting tackles made from the side by opponents.

Let us say the player is running directly at his opponents goal and a player makes a run and tackle at the ball from the side. Just preceding the moment of impact the ball is dragged back towards the possessing player using the sole of the foot. Hopefully the tackling player will have missed the ball and overshot his mark. The sole is rolled down the back of the ball which is then pushed forward with the inside ball of the foot.

1 Forward dribble using inside or outside of the foot.

2 As the player makes his attack from the side the sole is placed on top of the ball. The foot has been extended forwards to make this contact and will now drag the ball backwards to the rear of the standing foot. The action will stop when the foot has rolled right down the back of the ball to the ground.

3 Hopefully the opponent will have missed the ball and travelled across the front of the player in possession. At this point the ball is pushed forward with the inside ball of the foot.

4 The skill should be practised with a push-drag-push rhythm.

18 THE PELÉ

AERIAL DRIBBLE

This is a dribble where, instead of going round players with the ball, it is knocked over their heads and controlled on the other side of them, maintaining mobility throughout. The obstacles (players) can be real or imaginary, they are best shown by markers to give the exercise discipline.

1 Knock the ball up from a pull and flick up. (See Juggling Skill number 1.)

2 Get several aerial touches in before using the technique for the mobile juggle described in Juggling Skill number 19.

3 At the first obstacle knock the ball just over the top. Where the player is imaginary, play the ball at a height above your own. Do not hit it too high as this will make control more difficult and you will have to wait longer for the ball to descend.

4 If you are concentrating on one foot when controlling the ball on the other side of the obstacles (opponent), then run to the opposite side of the controlling foot when you pass your opponent, e.g., right foot control-run to your left when rounding your opponent.

5 The technique for applying backspin to balls controlled in the air with the upper foot (Juggling Skill number 15) will help to absorb the pace of the dropping ball.

6 Pace can be absorbed by using the thigh on the other side of the obstacle.

9 THE BLISSETT

This skill is similar to the Rossi in the first stage but when the foot has passed over the ball from inside to outside it is the outside of the other foot which comes across to take the ball in the opposite direction to the dummy.

1 **The player is chest on to the ball with the ball in front of the dummying foot.**

2 **The dummying foot passes explosively over the top of the ball from inside to outside.**

3 **The dummying foot must pass further to the outside of the ball than it did for the Rossi and the body must lean and transfer weight to that foot.**

4 **The other foot is brought across so that the ball can be swept in the opposite direction to the dummy using the outside surface.**

20 THE ZICO

GLIDE DUMMY

A great skill where the player approaches a pass across its line of play. The nearest foot glides over the ball impassively and the furthest foot plays the ball with the inside surface in the direction of the glide.

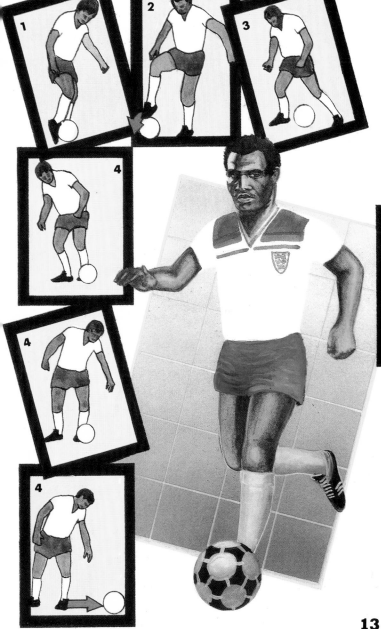

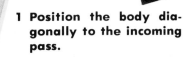

1 **Position the body diagonally to the incoming pass.**

2 **Move to the pass across its line of progress.**

3 **Play the nearest foot over the top of the ball in a casual manner.**

4 **The ball will pass through to the inside surface of the other foot which plays the ball quickly in the direction of the original glide.**

2. PACE ABSORBERS AND TRAPS

1 THE ROMERO
TOP FOOT PACE ABSORBER

The first principle of getting the body into the flight path of the ball applies to this skill. It can be used when the ball has a direct trajectory and when it has been hit with pace, because we are arresting the impetus of the ball and not trying to catch it.

1 **Get the body in line with the descent of the ball, or align leg and foot to the flight path.**

2 **Extend the control surface towards the ball.**

3 **On impact withdraw the playing surface, using it as a brake.**

4 **Just before the controlling foot reaches the ground the toes are pointed downwards to deliver the ball to the ground.**

2 THE ROMERO
TOP FOOT CATCH

In this skill the ball is caught between the upper surface of the toes and the shin. The foot is raised to the ball and relaxed on impact to absorb the pace, making it possible to clamp the ball before the controlling foot touches the ground.

1 **In the formative stages the ball should not drop from a great height.**

2 **It is important that the catching surface and the ball are in line.**

3 **The foot should be lifted to the dropping ball.**

4 **At the point of impact it should be relaxed with the ball to absorb the pace.**

5 **Before the foot is lowered the upper foot should be snapped back towards the shin clamping the ball.**

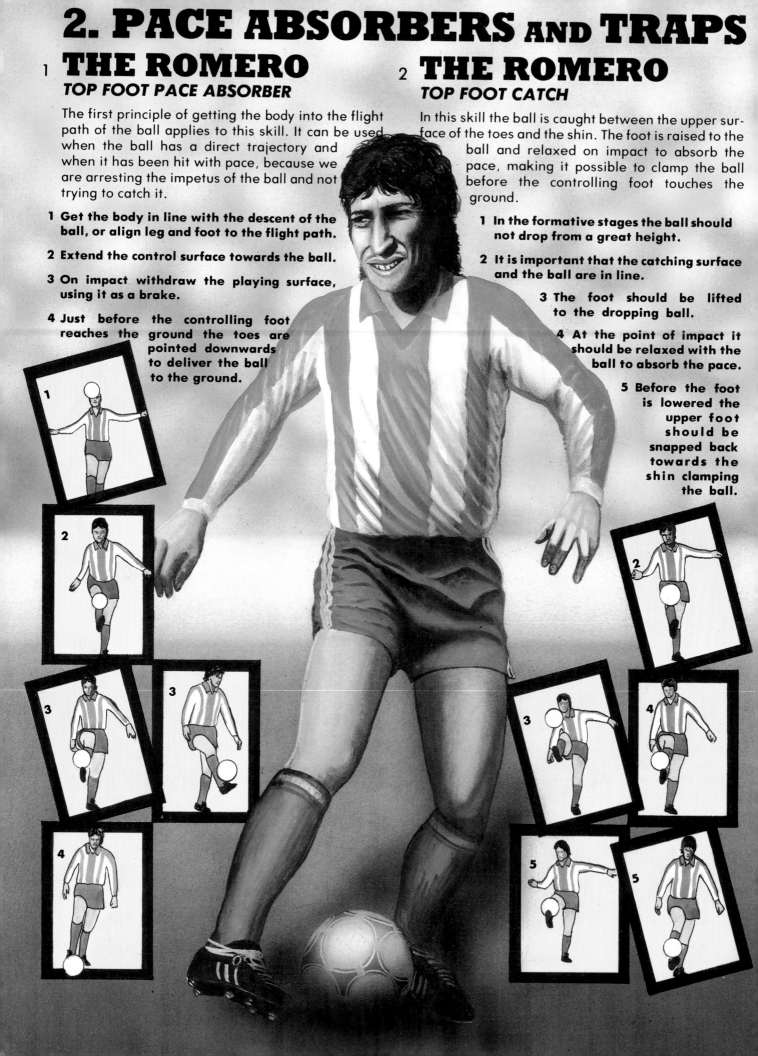

3 THE BONIEK

This skill is performed when the ball has a gradual descent. The ball is taken from the air and guided down between the players legs ready for him to turn and take control of.

1 The body has to be in the line of flight of the ball.
2 The controlling surface is extended towards the ball after the standing leg has kicked upwards in a scissor movement.
The playing surface is relaxed upon impact guiding the ball down, acting as a brake, inside the standing leg which has not yet reached the ground.
4 The ball is allowed to drop off the playing foot when it has reached a point behind the standing foot which has been thrown forward.
5 The player then turns and moves off with the ball.

4 THE BONIEK

In this sequence the top foot catch is executed from a bounced ball using the method described in the pace absorbers and traps section Skill number 2. Stability and good balance must be achieved before the transfer from one foot to another is attempted.
Once the ball has been trapped by the first foot it is thrown upwards from the foot to a distance of about eighteen inches. The second foot is taken up to the ball and on contact relaxed with the balls descent and pincered against the shin. This can be done continuously once a rhythm has been established.
This skill can be performed with forward movement, the player trying to reach a target with the ball controlled in this fashion. This skill once perfected is guaranteed to infuriate your manager.

1 The catching foot is lifted to the dropping ball.

2 Once the ball has been trapped by the catching foot it is thrown upwards

and over in the direction of the second foot.

3 The second foot is now taken up to the ball and on contact held against the shin.

CATCH TRAP TRANSFERRED TO OTHER FOOT

4 You are now ready to transfer the ball back to the first foot.

5 THE FRANCIS
CROSS-LEGGED OUTSIDE FOOT TRAP

In this trap the controlling foot passes across the front of the standing foot. The ball is trapped with the outside of the foot and swept across the standing foot. The ball can be trapped and left at its original point of impact. This skill is particularly good for screening and keeping distance between an opponent and the ball.

1 **The chest is square on to the flight path of the ball. The trapping leg is swept across the standing leg just below the knee.**

2 **The outside area of the instep is used to control the ball.**

3 **The higher the surface of the ball addressed the more complete the trap. This is the best method when the ball is being left at its original point of impact. Where the ball is being swept across the standing foot it should be played just below the horizontal mid-line of the ball.**

6 THE BECKENBAUR
INSTEP TRAP AT THE BACK OF THE STANDING FOOT

The dropping ball is controlled by the inside surface of the instep. The controlling leg crosses behind the standing foot. The trapping foot is turned with the toes pointing towards the standing foot with the heel uppermost.

1 **At the time of contact with the ball the chest is diagonal to the flight path of the ball.**

2 **The trapping leg is bent at the knee and crossed behind the standing foot with the toe on the ground and the heel held approximately six inches off the ground. The standing foot is turned diagonally away from the area of control.**

3 **The arch of the foot with the heel held off the ground presents a trapping area for the ball to be controlled in.**

4 **The degree to which the ball is 'killed' or allowed to partially escape is determined by the angle of the heel, e.g., where the heel is upright in relation to the toes the ball will escape with back spin, where the heel is forward and inclined the ball will be trapped decisively.**

5 **Escape is a useful component where the ball requires redirection, e.g., to bring the ball round the standing foot to the original position of the trapping foot.**

THE MUHREN
OUTSIDE FOOT TRAP AT THE BACK OF THE STANDING FOOT

This skill is identical to the previous skill in every way except that the final controlling surface is different. Instead of trapping the ball with the inside of the foot the outside surface of the foot is brought down on the ball to control it.

1 At the time of contact with the ball the chest is diagonal to the flight path of the ball.

2 The trapping leg is bent at the knee and crossed behind the standing foot. The foot is held off the ground with the toe pointing away from the standing foot.

3 The foot is pointed downwards and the area between the laces and the outside of the ball of the foot is the controlling surface.

4 The ball can be killed by rotation at the ankle, bringing the lace area of the instep more directly over the top of the ball. 'Escape' is achieved by using the outside of the foot.

5 To redirect the ball around the standing foot the side of the foot is placed lower down the ball at the horizontal mid-line.

THE MUHREN
CONCAVE CHEST TRAP

The shoulders are brought forward and the back is rounded producing an absorbent surface at the chest. The trunk is tilted forward and the ball directed downwards. This technique is best used when the incoming ball is rising or coming directly to a player.

1 Get in the flight path of the ball and be ready to adjust your height. The chest needs to be over the ball. This may mean having to jump or bend at the knees.

2 The chest is extended towards the ball. On impact the shoulders are snapped forward to produce an absorbent surface for the ball to hit.

3 At the same time as you snap the shoulders forward the trunk is tilted forward directing the ball downwards.

4 The greater the degree of tilt by the trunk the closer to the feet the ball will land.

9 THE CZERIATYNSKY

CONVEX CHEST TRAP WITH BALL ROLLING DOWN BODY

The ball has to be trapped by the chest in such a way to prevent it bouncing from the player. We have in the first place to stick the chest out and then, on impact, to produce an excess of flesh and muscle by snapping the shoulders and arms forwards. The back should be arched to present a platform for the ball to roll off of and down the body to the thigh.

1 Get in the line of flight of the ball.

2 Extend the chest towards the ball, at the same time as arching the back to provide a platform for the ball to fall on to. The chest should be stuck out with the shoulders back.

3 On impact the shoulders are snapped back, still retaining the arched back.

4 Where a player has jumped or gone on to tip-toe this will all help to absorb the pace as the player returns to the ground.

5 Straightening of the back will cause the ball to roll off the chest and down to the thigh, the upper foot or the ground.

10 THE SANTIN

GLUTEUS MAXIMUS TRAP

This skill can be employed when the ball approaches the player from the rear whether directly or diagonally. The ball must have a steep descent for the skill to be practicable. The ball is trapped after it has bounced and begun to rise, by the players posterior being placed above the ball to prevent its escape.

1 The ball is controlled in this fashion when it approaches the player from the rear.

2 The steeper the descent the closer the player has to be to the point where the ball bounces. Where the descent is shallow the player does not have to be so close. Experimentation will clarify the positions that need to be taken up in relation to the trajectory of the incoming ball.

3 Flexion takes place at the knee joint lowering the fleshy area at the top of the thigh towards and over the rising ball.

4 The fleshiness of the controlling surface will be sufficient to absorb the momentum of the ball and return it to the ground ready for the ensuing skill.

THE OLSEN
THIGH BOUNCE

The thigh bounce is a delivery skill, in that the surface is used to project the ball to other surfaces for ensuing skills. The fleshy part of the thigh is used to control and divert the dropping ball to the feet or the chest, or to team-mates in close attendance.

1 The player should be in a direct line with the ball for good balance, under stress he may line the controlling surface up with the ball without movement of the whole body.

2 The controlling surface should be moved to the ball at a speed commensurate with the degree of bounce required, i.e., the faster the thigh action and the more follow through then the further and quicker the ball will travel.

3 The ball can be bounced to the chest by using follow through. The extent to which this is used will be determined by the speed and trajectory of the incoming ball.

4 To divert a ball to the side of a player, the thigh will be rotated at the hip to the appropriate side.

5 This skill should not be confused with the Thigh Trap where withdrawal of the playing surface takes the pace off the ball.

THE OLSEN
BACK-SPIN CHIP AND DUMMY THROUGH THE LEGS

This skill has two essential criteria; one, that the incoming ball is on the ground; two, that the ball is at medium or medium to fast pace. When the ball approaches the player is is struck centrally to produce anti-clockwise spin. The returning ball is allowed to pass between the players legs, and he turns to the left or the right to collect the ball and proceed.

1 The ball is received on the ground at medium or fast pace. Anything slower will not produce sufficient spin for the skill to be viable.

2 When the ball approaches the playing foot the player stabs centrally beneath the ball with the toes producing anti-clockwise spin which causes the ball to rotate back towards the player.

3 The player allows the ball to pass between his legs before swivelling on whichever foot he chooses and collecting the ball with his back to its original point of service.

4 Where the player has used his right foot and turns to the left, the controlling surface on completion of a half turn will be the inside of the right foot: where the player turns to right, the controlling surface will be the outside of the right foot.

19

INSIDE FOOT RIDE

This skill is ideal for controlling direct passes at a player whether on the ground or up to two feet off it. The inside of the foot is used to take pace off the ball and to act as a break taking the ball through at a controlled pace past the standing foot which pivots so the player can be facing the now dead ball.

1 **The controlling foot is turned out so that the inside surface of the instep is presented squarely to the ball.**

2 **The surface is extended to the oncoming ball and on impact, is withdrawn, riding the ball close to the controlling foot and past the standing foot.**

3 **The player now pivots on the standing foot so as to complete a half turn.**

4 **The ball by now should have stopped or slowed and the player is ready to apply the next skill.**

BACK SPIN WITH THE BALL CIRCLING OUTSIDE THE PLAYER

This skill is best performed when the ball is on the ground travelling at medium pace. The player moves to the ball, dummies to kick it diagonally in the direction from whence it came, then strikes through the extreme inside of the ball slicing it and applying extreme spin. The ball will spin back around the player for him to turn and collect.

1 **Move to the ball sideways on, chest facing the direction which is opposite to the intended route of the ball.**

2 **Slice through the extreme inside of the ball causing the ball to spin outwards rotating in the direction the ball will take.**

3 **The player has two options when it comes to turning. Firstly he can turn away from the spin and possibly round his opponent, or he can take the same route as the ball hoping that the initial dummy has caused the opponent to move to the opposite side.**

4 **The foot surface to be used is the extreme outside of the little toe and the outside ball of the foot.**

THE ARCHIBALD

BALL THROUGH THE LEGS AND INSIDE FOOT TURN

When the ball is passed on the ground the player, who turns his back to the ball, dummies to kick the ball with the outside of his foot. This passes over the ball to produce the effect of the ball going between his legs. At this point the ball is turned inwards using the inside of the foot.

1 Just before receiving the ball the player turns his back to the ball.

2 He passes the playing foot over it, pretending to kick it with the outside of the foot.

3 The ball will roll between the dummying foot and the standing foot. At this point it is turned inwards across the front of the standing foot, using the inside of the instep.

THE ARCHIBALD

OVERHEAD CHIP-KICK

This technique is best performed when the ball is static and from set pieces. It particularly lends itself to the free kick situation where a well-constructed wall has been formed. The player taking the kick approaches the ball as though to try and play beyond the wall. He has his own player behind him. He chips the ball in the manner described below to bring the ball straight back over his own head, ready for a colleague to volley or half volley at goal.

1 **Approach the ball in a way that totally conceals your intentions.**

2 **Point the toe downwards and get the foot as far under the ball as possible.**

3 **The ball is lifted with an action similar to that of pedalling a bicycle backwards. The leg is fairly straight as the action begins, but bends increasingly at the knee as the ball is lifted higher.**

4 **To facilitate clearance over the player's head the player needs to lean backwards as much as possible.**

3. SHOOTING & PASSING

1 THE ROBSON
BENT GROUND SHOT (INSIDE FOOT)

We bend passes or shots for three reasons. Firstly to get the ball round obstacles such as a well positioned opponent. Secondly to turn the ball in the direction

we want a team mate to run, and thirdly to make it increasingly difficult for opponents to anticipate the trajectory of our shots or passes. In this skill we make the ball spin in an anti-clockwise direction by kicking the extreme outside of the ball with the inside instep area of the foot.

1 **From dead ball situations and for extreme spin the approach should start from a position well inside the position of the ball. This enables the back outside area of the ball to be hit. On the run when extreme spin is required the foot has to be moved diagonally across in relation to body position, to compensate for being directly behind the ball.**

2 **For ground shots or passes the ball needs to be kicked through the horizontal mid-line and to the extreme outside of the vertical line. The foot surface for this kick is the inside instep at the base of the big toe.**

3 **The line of follow through depends on the degree of spin we are trying for. Limited spin requires the foot to follow through the side of the ball while extreme spin requires a diagonal follow through more to the** back of the ball.
Players should familiarize themselves with the relationship between power, spin and distance, e.g., when we hit a ball with X amount of power and address the ball at a particular point what is the curve of the ball and is it sufficient to round a wall standing at 10 metres and enter a goal at 35 metres?

2 THE ROBSON
BENT GROUND SHOT (OUTSIDE FOOT)

The three reasons for bending the ball, mentioned in the previous skill, apply equally to this skill. There are three differences between this skill and the previous one; firstly the angle of approach, secondly the foot surface used and thirdly the area of the ball to be kicked.

1 **From a dead ball situation the angle of approach varies for the degree of spin required. For limited spin the approach will come from directly behind or just outside the line of the ball and its target. For extreme spin the player will approach from a point further outside this line.**

2 **So as to keep the ball low it should be struck just above the horizontal mid-line surface of the ball. For extreme spin the outside surface to the back of the ball should be struck.**

For limited spin the ball should be struck along the extreme outside.

3 **The surface area of the foot should be the outside area of the instep between the base of the little toe and the laces.**

4 **The standing foot should be behind the ball to allow the diagonal follow through.**

THE DIAZ
BENT VOLLEY (OUTSIDE FOOT)

This volley is hit with the outside of the foot with the player in the upright position.

1 From a served ball which should be descending the player should allow sufficient distance between himself and the ball for the kicking action to be unfolded.
2 Repeat component (2) of previous skill.
3 The ball should be struck on the extreme inside. Where distance and height is required it should be struck on the outer underside. Where a direct trajectory is required the ball should be struck through the horizontal mid-line to the extreme outside.

THE DIAZ
BENT VOLLEY (INSIDE FOOT)

The volley is a precise skill and especially so with the additional complication of swerve. The ball is struck while still in the air, and struck through the outside surface of the ball with the upper inside surface of the instep to produce anti-clockwise spin causing the ball to follow a curve. We are dealing here with the volley hit with the upright body stance or with nominal lean away from the ball. The lean-away volley is a separate skill.

4 The contact area of the foot is the outside of the foot at the base of the small toe.
5 For limited spin the foot will have a straight line down the outside of the ball. For extreme spin it will follow a diagonal path finishing to the outside of the standing foot.

1 The ball should be served from a throw and the ball, which is descending at the time of impact, will facilitate the straight stance. Fall-away techniques are usually applied to overcome the rising ball.

2 There are various adjustments that can be made to compensate for various heights or trajectories of the incoming ball. If the ball has dropped to a low level the leg can be fully extended at the time of impact. When the ball is high the upper leg needs to be flexed at the hip joint and the kicking action initiated at the knee joint.
3 The ball should be struck on the extreme outside.

Where height and distance are required the ball should be struck on the underside with the foot following through. Where the ball is to be kept low it should be struck to the outside of the horizontal midline and the toes pointed downwards.

4 The upper inside area of the instep at the base of the the big toe is the striking surface.

5 THE SIMONSEN

SWERVING THE HALF VOLLEY (INSIDE FOOT)

This skill differs from the others in that there is a critical moment of contact which cannot be recovered by compensatory action; e.g., if the contact is not made as the ball strikes the ground all sorts of malfunctions may occur. The ball must be struck through the extreme outside, producing anti-clockwise spin.

1 **The player must position himself for the moment when the ball hits the ground. The ball may come straight, or diagonally from either side, or even travel over the player from behind and this skill is still practicable.**

2 **The great danger is overlift, so the player must not be too far from the ball when it lands, nor must he lean back and make contact with a fully extended leg. The standing foot can be behind the ball but not so far behind it as to make full leg extension necessary. The optimum position is with the toes of the standing foot alongside the back of the ball, with the knee over the ball and the foot pointed downwards.**

3 **The foot surface is the inside area of the instep at the base of the big toe.**

4 **The ball should be struck through the outside of the horizontal mid-line where the ball needs to be kept low, with the knee over the ball, and slightly beneath this point where height is required.**

5 **Great spin can be produced by hitting the ball further round to the back.**

6 THE SIMONSEN

SWERVING THE HALF VOLLEY (OUTSIDE FOOT)

The ball must be struck as it hits the ground. The ball is struck through the side which is opposite to the previous skill using the outside of the upper foot between the laces and the base of the little toe.

1 **As previous Skill number 5.**

2 **The standing foot is behind the ball and the kicking foot addresses the extreme inside of the ball.**

3 **The foot surface used is the outside of the upper foot between the laces and the base of the big toe.**

4 **If the ball is to be kept low the knee should be over the ball at the momement of impact.**

5 **As previous Skill.**

THE TARDELLI
SCISSORS OVERHEAD KICK

A spectacular method of kicking which enables shots to be taken when a player is facing the wrong way and hasn't the time or space to turn. The objective before making a scissors kick is to get the feet into the position at present occupied by the head. This is achieved by allowing the body to fall away backwards, at the same time as we initiate a dynamic upward swing by the non-kicking leg from the hip joint. When the non-kicking leg is as high as the ball it is brought down to be replaced by the kicking leg swinging in the opposite direction. The ball is kicked backwards over the players shoulder, which needs to be lower than the kicking foot.

1 **The player should be beneath the ball with his back to the target. The legs should be bent at the knees ready for the upward thrust.**

2 **The jump is initiated off the non-kicking foot. The process of making the trunk fall away backwards and the upward launching of the non-kicking foot occur simultaneously. The fall back is impassive while the upward thrust of the legs is dynamic. This results in the legs going slightly further than the horizontal point and the trunk staying slightly below it.**

3 **The mechanics of the kick will depend on the position of the body in relationship to that of the ball. If, on reaching maximum height the ball is still at a distance then the leg is extended and power is initiated from the hip.**

If, however, the ball is close to the kicking foot flexion will take place at the knee though power will still come from forward rotation at the hip joint.

4 **It is essential to have some awareness of how you are going to fall since there is the danger of injury.**

THE TARDELLI
SHOT OR PASS FROM BEHIND THE STAND FOOT

A dynamic skill which will take opponents by surprise because of its speed and unorthodoxy. When a player is already stationed at the side of the ball he must jump off both feet, but upon landing the kicking foot must have crossed behind the standing foot. It is then brought explosively swinging at the knee joint to make contact with the ball. Where the player is mobile the same action takes place.

1 **Both feet need to be inside the ball if the line of the shot is to be straight; this is not necessary if the ball is to travel diagonally across the front of the player. The chest must face the target at the point of impact whether the shot is diagonal or straight. The arms play a big part in swinging the trunk when the shot is diagonal.**

2 **For the straight shot the feet, before the jump, need to be level with the back end of the ball. The standing foot, however, needs to have its toes level with the far side of the ball at the moment of impact. For the diagonal shot the standing foot can afford to be a couple of inches further back because the swivel compensates by allowing the kicking leg to come further round the standing leg, which swivels to point at the target.**

3 **Two surfaces are available and can be used to suit the position of the player at the time of kicking.**

The toe can be used by driving it beneath the line of the ball. The alternative surface to this, if the player has got close to the ball, is the instep surface close to the base of the toes. The toes should be on the ground at the moment of impact bringing the instep higher up the ball.

9 THE HODDLE

SHOULDER SHOT OR PASS

A rarely used ploy, which is surprising in view of its power and deceptiveness. When the ball is travelling towards you at great speed you do not always have the time to select ideal playing surfaces, therefore an ancillary range of skills is extremely important.

1 The player should be chest on to the oncoming ball. The feet should be apart to aid balance. Preceding impact the striking shoulder is withdrawn away from the ball before being thrust forward with as much speed as possible.

2 The bony area at the front of the shoulder is the contact surface.

3 The ball should be struck through the horizontal and vertical mid-lines of the ball.

4 The shoulder can be used to lob the ball at the same time as propelling it forward by combining an upward movement with the forward movement, thereby getting height as well as distance. The shoulder can be used for juggling the ball as a specific skill or incorporated in an integrated routine. See juggling section Skill number 23.

10 THE HODDLE

BACK-SPIN CHIP

The chip is used to gain early height over opponents and back spin helps in acquiring this. Back spin refines the skill in slowing the ball up as it falls to the ground. The foot strikes beneath the ball, without follow through taking place as for the drive. When Hoddle uses this skill, a great deal of the elevation comes from flexion taking place at the hip joint at the moment of impact, leaving the thigh in a horizontal position at the end of the skill (i.e. straightening at the knee never takes place).

1 Approach can be direct or angled. Here we are dealing with the direct approach.

2 The standing foot is placed to the side of and behind the ball.

3 The kicking foot stabs beneath the ball with the toes and base of the instep.

4 Using the Hoddle technique, the skill is viable even where the ground is hard. When the toes and then the instep are beneath the ball the leg remains bent at the knee with the leg completing a half-circle of backward rotation at the hip.

5 Where distance is required, straightening at the knee will be necessary, and on a dry ground height will be lost using this technique.

26

THE BUTRAGUENO

HEEL PASS AT RIGHT ANGLES TO PLAYERS RUN

An excellent skill for switching play, that preserves the element of disguise up to the last moment. The correct technique allows the ball to be struck cleanly and to remain on the ground.

1 The player making a straight run for an opponents goal may see the opportunity or necessity for a square pass.

2 For the sake of total deception, if the player is playing the ball with the outside of his foot and moving away from the direction of the intended pass, the playing foot must be switched from being turned inwards to being turned outwards, at right angles to the other foot. It is then brought across in a swinging action initiated at the knee, causing the ball to travel across the standing foot.

3 If the ball is to be kept low and the pass is fairly long, the horizontal and vertical mid-lines should be aimed for.

THE GIRRESSE

HALF VOLLEY, HEEL SHOT OR PASS

This skill is best used when the player is facing away from his target and when the ball is approaching his back or dropping vertically. It requires precise timing for contact to concur with the balls impact with the ground.

1 When the ball is approaching from behind a player and there is no time to turn, the kicking leg is flexed at the knee ready for the balls arrival.

2 The thigh is lifted slightly and the leg bent at the knee. The kicking leg sweeps across the standing leg, leverage taking place at the knee and striking with the heel through the horizontal mid-line of the ball.

13 THE LINEKER

SLING SHOT OR PASS FROM CAUGHT BALL

The first action (The Top Foot Catch) is described in the trapping section number 2.

Unless the performer is blessed with lithesome toes and a very long foot the ball is best controlled from a short drop, e.g., off the thigh. Once the ball has been caught the leg is withdrawn, still clasping the ball and thrust forward explosively, releasing the ball before the forward action has expired.

1 The ball should be caught in the manner described in the pace absorbers and trapping section number 2.

2 With the ball clasped between the upper surface of the toes and the shin it is held with the thigh just below the horizontal point. The leg is drawn back,

3 The foot is then thrust forward explosively with leverage at the knee.

4 Just before release the foot is pointed and the ball rolled to the upper toe surface. This gives the shot trajectory and extra power.

14 THE LINEKER

PASSING WITH THE OUTSIDES OF BOTH FEET (REVERSE SIDES)

For many reasons the technique of controlling the ball with the outside surface of the foot is superior. The foremost advantage is that it places maximum distance between an opponent and the ball. It enables mobility between control and subsequent movement. This exercise is excellent for developing physical co-ordination and mental alertness. If the ball comes to the receiving players left it is returned by the outside surface of the right foot. If the ball comes to the players right side it is returned with the outside surface of the players left foot.

1 Have a partner to serve the ball to you at medium pace or play the ball off a wall.

2 When the ball approaches to your left side the right foot should cross over to return the pass with the outside surface of the foot at the base of the little toe.

3 When the ball comes to your right side the left foot should cross over to return the pass with the outside surface as described in (2).

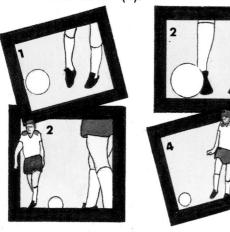

4 At the time of passing the body is slightly diagonal to the intended line of the pass.

5 There is very little follow through in the kicking action.

THE MARADONA

REVERSE SIDE CONTROL AND REVERSE SIDE PASS

When the ball is travelling towards the left side of the player he crosses his right foot over to control with the outside area of the instep, bringing the ball across to a position outside the natural position of the right foot. He then crosses the left foot over and strikes the ball with the outside of the instep passing the ball back in the direction it came from. So, if the ball is to your left you control with the outside of the right foot. If the ball is to your right you control with the outside of the left foot. When the ball is controlled and brought across to your right you pass with the outside of your left foot.

1 **When the ball approaches to your left side, the right foot should cross over to take the pass with the outside surface of the foot, at the base of the little toe.**

THE MARADONA

THIGH SHOT OR PASS

All too often we may select a technique in a game situation which will be rendered impracticable by the actions of an opponent. The thigh shot or pass cannot hope to be compared in efficiency or power with the available range of foot shots or passes but where possession or opportunity is to be lost if we wait for the ball to reach the foot then the thigh shot or pass may well prove advantageous, even crucial. The ball is struck with the thigh when it has dropped to a point beneath the hips (it is lobbed when contact takes place above this point). This allows the thigh to be midway between the straight and horizontal position at the time of contact.

1 **Get beneath, and where possible in line with the flight path of the ball.**
2 **Where the ball comes in from the side and the shot is to be made in a forward direction the player should face the ball. The thigh is raised and brought across the standing leg with sideways rotation at the hip.**
3 **If the ball is played with the thigh at or above the horizontal position it will rise vertically. The ball should be allowed to fall beneath the hips so that contact can be made with the thigh between the straight and horizontal position.**

2 The ball should be swept across to the right hand side of the player in the same movement as taking pace off the pass, which is achieved by extending the controlling foot to the ball and withdrawing it on impact.

3 When the ball has been transferred to the right side the left foot is crossed over with the foot turned in. The ball is then struck with the outside instep in the direction it   came from.

4 Where the angle of the shot differs from the angle of the incoming ball, at the point of impact the player pivots on the standing foot, so that when the skill is completed he is facing the target.

4. JUGGLING SKILLS

The juggling section of this book differs from preceding sections in that the contents are not presented as specific tricks which players can add to their repertoires but are more in the nature of explorative, experimental excercises designed to improve and extend the responses which a player can make to the aerial ball and to increase the ways in which he can get the ball from the ground to the air.

They are enjoyable exercises and a legitimate part of the development aspects of any players' programme of work. I am not suggesting that our game should be characterized by their constant inclusion but having said that I would be delighted to see any player with the audacity to use them to advantage in the game situation.

1 *FLICK-UP FROM SOLE ROLL*

The most common method of getting the ball into the air, especially for a juggling movement.

The ball is pulled towards the player with the ball of the foot immediately on top of the ball, the sole rolls down the ball, spinning the ball backwards. At the point where the toe has finally left the ball's surface it is dug beneath the spinning ball and levered upwards launching the ball into flight.

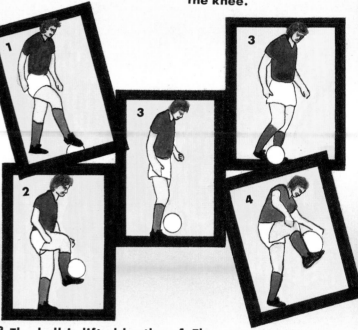

1 The ball is pulled back by the sole of the foot which is placed on the top of the ball.

2 The leg is flexed at the hip. Once the ball has been pulled back, flexion takes place at the knee.

3 The ball is lifted by the upper foot surface.

4 The movement comes from backward rotation of the hip, although the knee is still bent.

2 *TWO-FOOTED PINCER FLICK*

Another skill designed to get the ball off the ground keeping it close to the controlling player. The feet are placed either side of the ball and pointing outwards diagonally. They are snapped together swiftly causing the ball to rise upwards to about knee level.

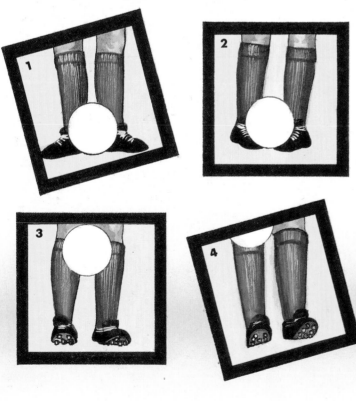

1 The feet should be placed either side of the ball with the centre of the ball level with the inside base of each big toe. The toes should be pointed diagonally outwards.

2 The soles should be slightly raised off the ground, throwing all the weight on to the heels.

3 The toes should now be snapped together in a fast powerful action beneath the ball with swivel taking place on the heels.

4 The ball will rise vertically upwards towards the knee cap and should be redirected by the upper foot to the next surface.

3 ONE-FOOT JUGGLE FROM FLICK-UP

For those learning the skill of juggling confidence is best gained and rhythm mastered by perfecting the art with ones natural foot. In this combination the ball is flicked up as described in Juggling Skill 1 and then juggled using the one foot, attempting a maximum number of consecutive touches without the ball touching the ground.

1 Flick up as in Juggling Skill 1.

2 Keep the ball airborne by keeping the foot at right angles to the leg thereby making a platform for the ball to hit.

3 The juggling leg should be bent at the knee and the ball kept close to the foot.

4 The number of touches without the playing foot touching the ground should be as few as possible since this places great strain on the player's balance.

5 Where the ball is played too high or deflected at a bad angle the skill should be started again rather than the player struggle to reassert control.

4 TWO-FOOTED JUGGLE FROM FLICK-UP

1 Flick up as in Juggling Skill 1.

2 With flexion at the hip and knee joint and the foot held horizontally balance and rhythm should be established with the good foot.

3 Transfer to the other foot should be effected not with a vertical ball but with a ball which is looped so as to fall vertically on to the other foot. Where this is not achieved body movement should take place so as to position the receiving foot beneath the dropping ball.

4 When confidence is gained the ball should be hit at varying heights and at varying speeds.

Progress to the use of two feet in keeping continuous aerial control should only be taken when some rhythm and balance with a player's best foot has been established. The same principles of leg position and foot surface apply. As an aid to negotiating the transfer from one foot to another, neither the receiving foot nor the ball wants to be too high. This obviates the risk of unwanted deflections and impaired balance.

5 ONE-FOOT CATCH JUGGLE

This juggle can be started in any way, i.e., bounced ball, thrown or flicked up. The ball is caught between the upper surface of the toes and the shin in a pincer action. The foot should be taken up to meet the dropping ball and relaxed at the moment of impact so as to ride with the ball. Having caught the ball it is thrown up by the holding foot and the movement is repeated again.

1 (Starting from flick-up.)
Flick the ball up as in Juggling Skill 1 with top foot until poise and balance is established.

2 At the optimum moment catch the ball as in Skill 2 (Pace Absorber and Traps).

3 The controlling foot is lifted upwards at the hip joint and the ball released from the pincer movement at the beginning of the upward stroke.

4 The controlling foot is raised to the descending ball and relaxed on impact so that the second catch can be effected.

5 These actions are repeated for as many catches as the player can make always trying to beat his previous best score.

6 Beware of balancing for too long on the standing foot alone. Try to make regular touch downs with the controlling foot to assist stability.

6 TWO-FOOTED CATCH JUGGLE

The mechanics described previously for the one foot catch juggle apply for this skill almost exactly except for the transfer from one side of the body to the other and this is the most difficult component. To catch a ball in this way when it is travelling from the side is extremely difficult. Therefore when the ball is thrown upwards from one foot it has also to be looped so as to fall directly to the new receiving foot.

1
As in Juggling Skill 5.

2
As in Juggling Skill 5.

3
As in Juggling Skill 5.

4
So that the ball drops directly for the new controlling foot it must be thrown upwards and across in a looping movement.

5
The receiving foot must be raised towards the transferred ball and relaxed on impact.

7 TOP-FOOT CATCH AND CARRY

The top foot catch has been described, and comprises the first part of this skill. When the ball has been securely caught between the upper surface of the toes and the shin, the player hops forward on the standing foot still clutching the ball. This skill will rarely be used in a competitive game, but is very useful for football tennis, squash etc.

1
Catch the ball as described in Skill 2 (Pace Absorbers and Traps).

2
The leg should be flexed at the knee with the thigh just below horizontal.

3
The player hops forward on the standing leg holding the ball in a top foot catch.

4
The player can hop backwards with the ball in a top foot catch.

8 THE SHOVEL LIFT

Different kinds of kicking technique produce different rates of ascent when we are kicking for height and where the ball is on the ground. The drive, for example, will rise more slowly than the chip. This skill is designed to bring about steep and immediate ascent from a dead ball situation or from the ball moving away from the player.

2
The playing foot should be placed beneath the ball. This is the component that distinguishes this skill from other kicking skills. The foot can approach the ball at speed but must be slowed down just before impact to prevent the ball being knocked forward.

1
The standing foot should be alongside the ball.

3
Once the toes are beneath the ball rotation at the hip and flexion at the knee will cause the ball to rise immediately.

4
When the ball has left the playing foot, the thigh should be in a horizontal position.

5
Forward movement of the ball can be achieved by straightening the leg.

9 THIGH JUGGLE

A ball tossed into the air by the player off the fleshy part of the thigh. Because the thigh is an absorbent surface the ball can be bounced quite high giving more time for correct position.

1 Throw the ball into the air just above the head.

Bring the thigh upwards to the horizontal position to make contact with the ball.

2 After each touch a natural standing position should be assumed and the thigh brought up to the horizontal position to make contact with the ball.

3 If the ball is played too early it will result in the ball coming back to the players chest, if the ball is played too late it will bounce away from the player, therefore the horizontal position of the thigh is the one to be aimed at.

4 As the player becomes more adept so the pace and height of balls played off the thigh should be varied.

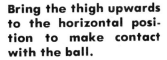

10 UPPER FOOT AND THIGH COMBINATION JUGGLE

This combination can be started from a dropped ball on to the thigh or from a flick-up on to the upper foot. Both skills have been dealt with individually. The important factor in this skill is that of transfer from one surface to the other. The player should, at first, attempt to get transfer from one surface to the other when the time is right, rather than follow a predetermined sequence.

1 Flick-up as in Juggling Skill 1.

2 The ball is played on the upper foot as in Juggling Skill 3.

3 Transfer from the foot to the thigh is best effected with flexion at the knee so that the ball follows a straight vertical line.

4 The player must ensure that the receiving surface (the thigh) is placed directly beneath the dropping ball.

5 Transfer from the thigh to the upper foot should be effected with a minimum of height off the thigh so as to make control easier for the upper foot.

11 THIGH AND FOOT CATCH JUGGLE

When attempting to catch a dropping ball on the upper foot it is often best to break the rate of descent of the ball with the thigh. In this combination skill the ball is passed from the thigh in a bounce, to be caught on the upper foot, balanced, then returned.

1 The use of the thigh surface has been comprehensively dealt with in this section and the mechanics so far described apply to this skill.

2 A relaxed and well-balanced thigh juggle should be set in motion ensuring that the controlling foot returns to the ground as often as possible.

3 The ball should be dropped from the thigh taking care not to produce too much height since this will make the catch more difficult.

4 The catching foot should be brought up to the ball and relaxed on impact when the pincer movement between the toes and the shin should be applied.

5 The ball should be held in this position and then thrown back up to the thigh.

12 *JUGGLE SPIN*

This skill is ideally suited to control of the ball which is descending but has a fairly direct trajectory. It is also a useful way of defusing the ball when the player is moving backwards. The pace is taken off the ball by applying backspin to the underside and rolling the ball backwards in this fashion.

1 **Line the chest up to the flight path of the ball.**

2 **Do not raise the playing foot any more than one foot off the ground, as this will restrict the movement required to produce the backspin. The leg should swing from the knee with the upper foot playing the underside of the ball.**

3 **The arms play an important part in maintaining balance and should be widespread. The player may be hopping backwards as he performs the skill so good balance is a critical feature.**

4 **The part of the foot at the base of the toes and the bottom of the instep is the controlling surface. This forms a cradle for the secure rotation of the ball. This skill is an ideal forerunner to the volley, the half volley or the lob.**

13 *SEQUENCE JUGGLES*

Sequence Juggling is where predetermined surfaces and numbers of touches are nominated before the performance of the routine. This is excellent training and discipline for controlling pace, direction and mental alertness.

1 **Begin by naming surfaces at which you know you are proficient, e.g., two touches right upper foot, two touches right thigh, two touches left thigh.**

2 **Rotate these surfaces in this order until you have mastered the technique of transfer between them with fluency.**

3 **Surfaces with which you are not so proficient should be the minority in any sequence until they become fully co-ordinated skills.**

4 **The target should be to combine surfaces in sequence which are furthest away from each other, e.g., right upper foot (two touches) to head (two touches) to left upper foot (two touches) to shoulder (two touches).**

5 **Further physical co-ordination and mental alertness is developed by varying the number of touches at each surface.**

14 *USING THE SHOULDER WITH OTHER JUGGLING SURFACES*

In this juggling section we have described how to use the upper foot, thigh, chest and head as well as the shoulder to keep the ball in flight and under control. It is best at first not to decide on which particular surfaces are to be used but to play to those surfaces which are appropriate to the position of the ball at the time of transfer. The component section will show a selection of surfaces as a suggestion rather than an arbitrary sequence.
(Top foot, thigh and shoulder).

1 **All the components for this combination are to be found elsewhere in the juggling section. There are certain demands imposed by transfer between the surfaces which will be dealt with now as components.**

2 **Transfer from upper foot to shoulder requires sufficient height for the ball to drop directly on to the playing surface.**

3 **Transfer from thigh to shoulder must have the** same height and descent patterns as for the upper foot.

34

5 MOBILE ONE-FOOTED JUGGLE

Juggling with the upper foot is the most popular form of exploratory soccer practised today, primarily because it is the easiest and most straight forward. It is surprising nonetheless how many players cannot master the rhythm and co-ordination essential for this skill, especially when mobility is required. The idea is to keep the ball in the air using the upper foot at the same time as moving forward.

1 **Start from a bounced ball rather than a dropped ball. This will make initial control easier.**

2 **The foot is held in the horizontal position while the leg is slightly flexed at the knee.**

3 **Control is made easier if the ball is not played too high.**

4 **Forward movement initially should be restrained to a walk and gradually sped up as the technique is mastered.**

5 **Return the kicking foot to the ground after each touch.**

6 **Never try to recover badly struck balls — start again.**

7 **Keep a score of the number of touches made without the ball touching the ground so that progress can be measured.**

6 TWO-FOOTED MOBILE JUGGLE

This is the logical progression from the previous skill. The components described there apply here. There is added difficulty in this skill caused by transfer of the ball from one foot to the other and also the use of the weaker foot.

1 **A reasonable standard of proficiency will have been reached in the previous skill before proceeding to this one; therefore the juggle can be started from a flick-up or a dropped ball.**

2 **The ball should be transferred from one side to the other in a diagonal loop enabling forward progress to be made at the same time as allowing the ball to drop on to the other foot.**

3 **The lower the ball is kept the more touches there will be over a given period but the higher a ball is played, the more difficult will be control at each touch.**

4 **Back spin is a useful application in this skill, to keep the ball rotating back towards the player as he progresses, and in slowing the aerial flight of the ball.**

7 MOBILE THIGH JUGGLE

The skill description used for the previous juggle applies to this skill except that the ball comes off the thigh slightly forward of vertical and the lean-back is emphasised.

1 **To make the ball bounce slightly forward of the vertical position contact has to be made before the thigh reaches a horizontal plane.**

2 **After each contact the player moves forward to arrive with the thigh beneath the descending ball.**

3 **Control is made easier if the ball is not played too high.**

VARIATIONS

1 Greater control can be developed by following predetermined sequences: two touches left thigh, one touch right thigh, one touch left thigh, two touches right thigh.

2 Sensitive weighting of the ball can be achieved by varying the height of each bounce. This can also be put into a sequence independent of the previous sequence or linked to it.

3 Knock the ball high and well forward, sprint to get beneath it with the thigh surface and control.

18 MOBILE JUGGLE ALL SURFACES

The pinnacle of the juggling repertoire and only for those who have worked at and accomplished the various components which precede it. The routine is best set to a particular distance, e.g., using all surfaces over a distance of 50 metres. All surfaces means upper foot, thigh, chest, shoulder, head, and can be rounded off with a catch trap.

19 HEAD JUGGLE

Controlled heading of this kind develops the player's ability to understand pace, timing and direction as well as developing the player's capacity to cope with the vertically descending ball.

1   The head juggle can be started from a thrown ball or a flick up and a kick. Initially the thrown ball is better for establishing quick balance and rhythm.

2   The head should be angled backwards so that the forehead is presented as a platform to the dropping ball.

3   The player must keep his eyes on the ball at all times and keep his head directly beneath the line of descent.

4   For this skill power is generated by flexion at the knee joints causing upward movement of the whole body beneath the ball.

5   As an aid to pace and feel for the ball the player should vary the distance of each header, heading both for height and close control.

6   Try heading the ball in this way at the same time as moving towards a target.

7   Try heading for distance, sprinting to the dropping ball, and controlling with the head.

20 HEAD AND SHOULDER JUGGLE

The shoulder being a bony surface is not an ideal juggling platform. For this reason subtlety of touch needs to be developed. Experiment at first by dropping the ball towards the shoulder, dip the opposite shoulder down, bending at the hips. Providing no swivel has taken place at the hip the ball should pass over the head from side to side, i.e., towards the other shoulder. By repeating the motion in the opposite direction it will be possible to loop the ball to and fro between the two shoulders. The introduction of the head as an intermediary surface demands a more sensitive contact at the shoulders and greater co-ordination.

1   From a ball thrown just above the head the shoulder must be placed just beneath the line of descent.

2   Experimentation must take place as to the height produced by different degrees of dipping the opposite shoulder.

3   Beware of producing swivel at the hips as this will send the ball forward rather than directly over or on to the player's head.

4   Once a rhythm is established between the shoulders the head can be introduced by directing the ball from the shoulder to the forehead.

TWO-FOOTED FLICK-UP BETWEEN HEELS

The ball needs to be static or moving slowly. The player traps the ball between his heels and by throwing the legs backwards and upwards, and releasing the ball when lower legs have formed a V with the upper legs the ball is thrown over the player's head.

1 From a one footed take-off make a two footed landing with one foot placed on each side of the ball.

2 The inside instep towards the heels is clamped to each side of the ball.

3 The lower legs are now thrown upwards and backwards, lifting the ball between the feet.

4 When the lower legs form a V with the upper legs the ball should be released to travel over the player's head.

5 If the ball is released too early it is thrown out backwards. If it is released too late it hits the player's back.

2 FLICK-UP BETWEEN HEEL AND TOP FOOT

There are many ways of getting a dead ball into the air, and the pull and flick up has already been discussed. This method is a more complex skill demanding greater co-ordination but mastery of it will produce infinite fulfilment. The ball is trapped between the upper toes and instep of the back foot against the heel and achilles tendon of the front foot. The front foot then flicks the ball up, to the back of the player and over his head.

1 The ball can be still or rolling away from the player. Most players like to put their best foot forward but this is up to the individual.

2 Place the front foot in front of the ball.

3 As the heel of the front foot makes contact with the ball the upper toes and instep of the trailing foot must close with the back of the ball trapping it against the heel.

4 The front leg must now be flexed explosively towards the player's rear. He will have both feet off the ground at this stage.

5 The back foot only releases contact with

the ball once movement (4) has been initiated.

6 If the ball does not come over the player it could be due to two factors:
(a) the ball is not being

rolled high enough up the back of the front leg; (b) flexion at the knees is not fast enough.

3 HEAD CATCH AND NECK TRAP

The idea of this skill is to catch the ball on the forehead. As with the catch trap the playing surface is extended towards the ball and relaxed on impact. Invariably because of the hardness of the surface several touches are required to absorb the pace before the ball is finally rested on the forehead. Forward and downward movement of the head will cause the ball to roll over the back of the head. The ball is then caught in the cradle formed between the base of the head and the nape of the neck.

1 From a thrown ball the forehead surface should be relaxed on impact so as to absorb the pace. Several touches may be required to completely 'defuse' the ball.

2 The ball should be balanced on the forehead until it is still.

3 Forward rotation of the head now takes place

taking the chin down to the chest causing the ball to roll over the back of the head; the chin is then thrust forward, the shoulders snapped back and the trunk bent forwards at the hips, to form a cradle between the top of the spine and the nape of the neck, in which the ball can rest.

VARIATION
The ball can then be rolled down the back and kicked with the back of the heel over the players head to his front.

5. JUNIOR UNITS OF

SKILL DEVELOPMENT

1

1. Run with the ball using the inside of one foot. (An elementary technique not featured in this book.)
2. Stop the ball with the sole of the foot. (See Dribbling Skill No. 13, page 10.)
3. Pull the ball back in the opposite direction. (See Dribbling Skill No. 15, page 11.)
4. Dribble, using the outside surface of one foot. (See Dribbling Skill No. 14, page 10.)
5. Flick-up from sole roll and bend a half-volley at a large target with the inside instep. (See Shooting Skill No. 5, page 24.)

2

1. From a bounced ball, make four top foot touches without the ball hitting the ground. (See Juggling Skill No. 3, page 31.)
2. Two-footed juggle. Six touches, three each foot. (See Juggling Skill No. 4, page 31.)
3. From a dropped ball, control with a top foot pace absorber. (See Pace Absorber Skill No. 1, page 14.)
4. Perform the Keegan dummy over a fifteen metre dribbling run. (See Dribbling Skill No. 1, page 4.)

3

1. Kick the ball high and control with a thigh trap. (See Pace Absorber Skill No. 11, page 19.)
2. Three top-foot touches on each foot. (See Juggling Skill No. 4, page 31.)
3. From high ball, control with the head and juggle three times on the head.
4. Cross legged outside foot trap from dropped ball. (See Trapping Skill No. 5, page 16.)
5. One Rossi dummy over a fifteen metre run. (See Dribbling Skill No. 4, page 5.)

4

1. From a ball rolled along the ground at medium pace use the inside foot ride. (See Pace Absorber Skill No. 13, page 20.)
2. Sole of the foot control, pulling the ball in three different angles. (See Dribbling Skill No. 13, page 10.)
3. Stop the ball with the sole using two-footed pincer movement. (See Juggling Skill No. 2, page 30.)
4. Kick the ball above the head and control with a convex chest trap. (See Trapping Skill No. 9, page 18.)
5. From previous skill use top foot pace absorber. (See Pace Absorber Skill No. 1, page 14.)

5

1. From a thrown ball use a convex chest trap, to thigh, to top foot catch. (See Trapping Skills Nos. 2, 9, and 11.)
2. Run with the ball over 30 metres using sole roll technique (See Dribbling Skill No. 16.)
3. Return, using Ardiles. (See Dribbling Skill No. 16.)
4. Flick-up from sole roll to head, drop to the thigh, to upper foot and let the ball fall to the ground. (See Juggling Skills No. 1 and Pace Absorber Skills Nos. 11 and 1.)
5. Two-footed flick-up between heels, bringing the ball over the head and executing the bent volley with the inside of the foot. (See Shooting Skill No. 3.)

6. SENIOR UNITS

1

1. Flick up from sole roll. (See Juggling Skill No. 1, page 30.)
2. Two-footed juggle-five each foot. (See Juggling Skill No. 4, page 31.)
3. Thigh juggle-two each thigh. (See Juggling Skill No. 9, page 33.)
4. Top Foot Pace Absorber. (See Pace Absorber Skill No. 1, page 14.)
5. Perform one Ardiles over a 15 metre dribbling run. (See Dribbling Skill No. 16, page 11.)

2

1. Instep trap at the back of the standing foot from a thrown ball. (See Pace Absorber Skill No. 6, page 16.)
2. Perform one Keegan over a 15 metre dribbling run. (See Dribbling Skill No. 1, page 4.)
3. Take a bent ground shot with the inside of the foot at a target. (See Shooting Skill No. 2, page 22.)
4. From the rebound apply outside foot spin with the ball circling outside the player. (See Pace Absorber Skill No. 14, page 14.)
5. Perform one Dalglish over a 15 metre dribbling run. (See Dribbling Skill No. 17, page 18.)

3

1. From a thrown ball apply an instep trap at the back of the standing foot. Allow escape, bringing the ball round to the front of the standing foot. (See Trapping Skill No. 7, page 17.)
2. One-footed mobile juggle over 15 metres. (See Juggling Skill No. 15, page 35.)
3. Head juggle. Five touches. (See Juggling Skill No. 19, page 36.)
4. The Keegan and flick. (See Dribbling Skill No. 2, page 4.)
5. The Blissett. (See Dribbling Skill No. 19, page 13.)

4

1. From a thrown ball juggle spin, moving backwards.
2. From a thrown ball, two touch shoulder juggle. (See Juggling Skill No. 15, page 35.)
3. Cross-legged outside foot trap. (See Trapping Skill No. 5, page 16.)
4. Flick-up and catch trap. (See Juggling Skill No. 1, and Trapping Skill No. 2, pages 30 and 14.)
5. Kick the ball over the head and use top foot pace absorber. (See Pace Absorber Skill No. 1, page 14.)

5

1. Kick the ball, using the back of the standing foot technique. (See Shooting Skill No. 8, page 25.)
2. Step over and ride. (See Dribbling Skill No. 9.)
3. Chip the ball up for upper foot and thigh combination juggle.
4. One touch, both shoulders and head juggle. (See Juggling Skill No. 20, page 36.)
5. Swerve the half-volley (outside foot) at a target from 25 metres. (See Shooting Skill No. 6, page 24.)

6

1. From a thrown ball, use the top foot scissors trap with the ball going through the legs. (See Trapping Skill No. 3, page 15.)
2. Thirty metre dribbling run using both outside foot surfaces. (See Dribbling Skill No. 14, page 10.)
3. Two footed pincer flick. (See Juggling Skill No. 2, page 30.)
4. Both feet and both thighs mobile juggle over twenty metres. (See Juggling Skills Nos. 16 and 17, page 35.)
5. Convex chest trap with the ball rolling down the body. (See Skill No. 9, page 18.)

7

1. Two Rossi's over fifteen metres. (See Dribbling Skill No. 4.)
2. Flick-up between heel and top-foot. (See Juggling Skill No. 22.)
3. Thigh bounce and top foot catch. (See Pace Absorber Skills, Nos. 11 and 2.)
4. Top Foot catch and carry. (See Juggling Skill No. 7.)
5. Top foot control over fifteen metres pulling the ball through at four different angles. (See Dribbling Skill No. 13.)

8

1. Receive a ball played along the ground and perform the Conti turn. (See Dribbling Skill No. 9.)
2. Flick-up between heel and toe bringing the ball over the player's head. (See Juggling Skill No. 22.)
3. Three consecutive shoulder shots against a wall or from a thrown ball. (See Shooting Skill No. 9.)
4. Upper foot, thigh and head mobile juggle over twenty metres. (See Juggling Skills No. 19.)
5. Repeat, running backwards. (See Skills as above.)

9

1. The Keegan. (See Dribbling Skill No. 1.)
2. The Rossi with back foot drag. (See Skill No. 3.)
3. The Conti. (See Dribbling Skill No. 8.)
4. The Dalglish. (See Dribbling Skill No. 17.)
5. The Ardiles. (See Dribbling Skill No. 17.)

HEAD AND FOOT TENNIS

1
The court to be agreed by the players.

2
The number of players to be agreed. The size of the court should be taken into account when deciding on numbers.

3
The net should be about 2 metres from the ground.

1
The court should be stipulated by the coach or in his absence agreed between the players. Badminton, volley ball or basketball courts all have suitable dimensions.

2
The number of players to be agreed, though between four and six per side is a suitable number.

4
The ball can be served with the head from a forward section of the court or with a kick from the base line.

5
The number of bounces permitted should be agreed between the players and the ability of the players should be taken into account when deciding this.

6
Only one player may touch the ball with surfaces other than the head after which the ball must be played with the head.

7
The ball can be played with the head between players in their own court a predetermined number of times (e.g., three).

8
A point can only be awarded to the serving team.

3
The net should be about one and a quarter metres high.

4
Service is taken from the base line with a volley from a bounced ball.

5
The ball can be returned by any surface other than the hands.

6
For good players the game is more exciting if only one bounce is permitted. The number of bounces allowed should be determined by the overall ability of the players involved.

7
Each player may touch the ball only once before it is returned over the net.

8
A net point can only be awarded to the serving team.

PLEASE NOTE DIAGRAMS ARE NOT TO SCALE

ALL TOUCH TENNIS

1

The net is the same as that used for Football Tennis (Game No. 1).

2

A maximum of four players is recommended for this game.

3

Good players can play off one bounce while average players may need two or even three bounces.

4

When the ball has crossed the net every player in the side must touch the ball before it is returned.

5

All surfaces except the hands are allowed.

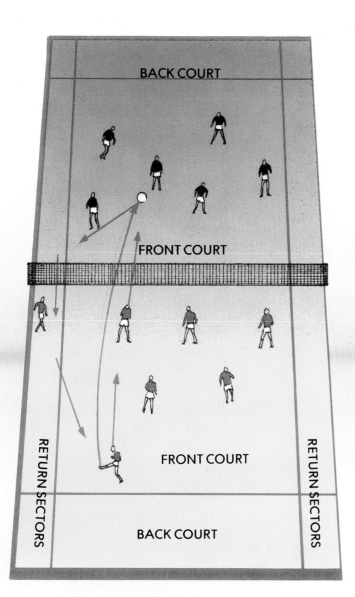

Hit and ....Run

1

The court dimensions are the same as for Football Tennis (Game No. 1). There should be two lines, one on each side of the net, dividing the front court from the back court. The back court will constitute one third of the playing surface on each side of the net.

2

The rules are the same except for the changes described in the next two rules.

3

The net should be one metre off the ground.

4

When a ball is played from a back court zone the player who played the ball must follow the ball, jumping the net and may try to stop his opponents playing the ball back. This includes the service which makes running automatic from the kick, running does not take place when a ball is played from the front court.

5

No physical contact is allowed and the use of the hands is barred. Feet must not be raised above the knee level in an attempt to block a return.

6

When a player returns to his own court he must do so along one side of the playing area.

7

Teams should concentrate on getting players into back court zones and to play high balls which give the runner more time to get into the opposing court.

SOCCER SQUASH

1
The court has to be agreed by the players concerned as does the wall surface. A suggested plan is shown on this page.

2
The number of bounces allowed before return should be agreed before the game and the ability of both players should be taken into account when deciding this.

3
The ball should be served from behind the agreed serving line from a dropped volley kick.

4
The ball can be returned without waiting for the bounces.

5
The ball can be juggled up to three times before it is played.

6
The ball must bounce inside the agreed boundaries.

7
When the ball is obviously going out of court but is played by an opponent and subsequently goes out this counts against the player who last played the ball.

8
Points are awarded regardless of service.

TARGET SQUASH

1
The dimensions and rules for this game are the same as for Soccer Squash (Game No. 5) except that three circles are drawn on the wall.

2
The centre one should have a diameter of half a metre while the outside ones should be one metre. A circle of one metre diameter should be placed on the floor two metres from the wall and central to the outer boundaries. The players should concentrate on hitting these targets which earn them bonus points.

3
If a player kicks a ball inside the centre circle he scores three bonus points. If he kicks it inside the two outer circles he scores two bonus points.

4
If he hits the centre circle on the wall and the ball on its first bounce falls in the circle on the ground he automatically wins the game.

5
Points are awarded regardless of service.

6
Where targets are missed the game continues to be scored in the normal way.

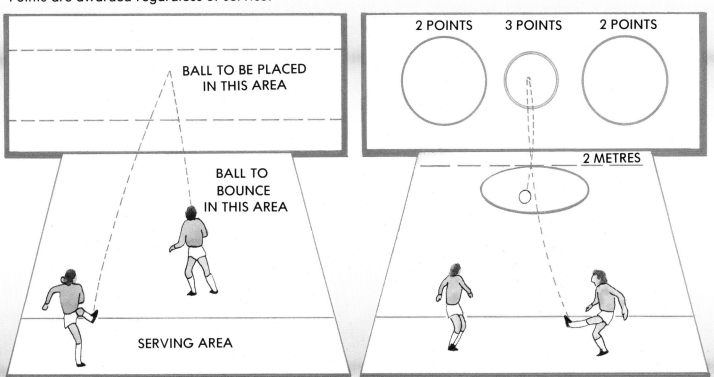

BALL TO BE PLACED IN THIS AREA

BALL TO BOUNCE IN THIS AREA

SERVING AREA

2 POINTS   3 POINTS   2 POINTS

2 METRES

BENCH FOOTBALL

1

Two teams should be selected. There should not be more than six in each.

2

They are placed in diagonally opposite corners of the hall or pitch.

3

The pitch should be about the size of a usual five-a-side pitch.

4

A bench is placed on its side with the seats facing into the pitch two yards in from each by-line.

5

The ball is placed in the centre of the pitch.

6

Each player on both sides is given a number from one to six.

7

The referee shouts a number and the player with that number sprints round the outside of the pitch past his opponents goal until he gets round to his own goal. He jumps over the centre of the bench and sprints for the ball. The other player will have jumped over the bench at the other end of the pitch.

8

The two players then try to score a goal by hitting their opponents bench. The pitch should be divided into quarters. To score, a player must pass into the last quarter of the pitch. This is to encourage the player to dribble and retain possession, as well as vary the pace. Where shooting practice is required this rule can be waived.

9

The referee can call more than one number. He may, at the end of the activity call six numbers.

10

When two players have failed to score over a long period, and fatigue has set in, the referee can call reinforcements.

11

Where the coach wants to condition a game by creating three vs. one or three vs. four situations he may point to the end when he calls a number. He must point to the end, which is to be in the minority, first.

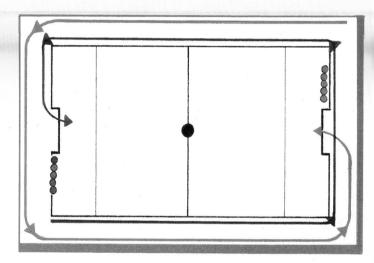

WALL JUGGLE

1

The ball is played against the wall from a bounce.

2

Once it has hit the wall it should be controlled by the other player and played back against the wall without touching the ground.

3

Each player is allowed two touches to control the ball before returning it to the wall.

4

Keep count of the strikes against the wall without the ball touching the ground.

5

This is essentially a co-operative and not a competitive exercise. The aim should be to produce situations which make it easier for your partner rather than difficult.

DRIVING LESSONS

1
The players stand 5 metres apart facing each other.

2
The player with the ball pushes it to his partner who pushes it back.

3
He then moves backwards and continues to move backwards while the ball is passed between himself and his partner.

4
When the player who is running forward changes his angle subsequent movement goes in a straight line from this point.

FLYING LESSONS

1
The two partners face each other about five metres apart.

2
One player holds the ball.

3
He lobs the ball to his partner who can return it using any surface other than the hands.

4
Having returned it, the player starts to move backwards.

5
Moving in this way the two players keep the ball in the air trying to reach a predetermined target.

A Juggle Swop

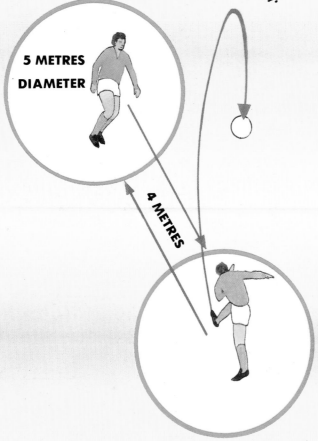

1
Both players stand in their own circle which should have a diameter of at least five metres.

2
The two circles should be four metres apart.

3
One player juggles with the ball until he has absolute control.

4
He then calls his partner's name and plays the ball vertically into the air.

5
The partner has to sprint to the other circle and endeavour to catch the ball before it hits the ground.

6
The partner who played the ball into the air has meanwhile sprinted to the other circle where he waits.

7
It is now the turn of the player who has controlled the ball to call his partner and play the ball into the air.

8
Scores should be kept of the number of successful rallies.

WALL HEAD BALL

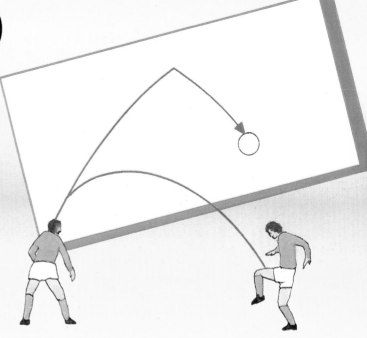

1
Both players stand facing a high wall. One of the players holding a ball.

2
The ball is thrown high against the wall.

3
The player who has not thrown the ball then heads the ball back against the wall.

4
Taking turns the two players try to keep the ball going between themselves and the wall.